Copyright © 2023 by Emiko Sarasawati Susilo.

All rights reserved. No part of this publication may be reproduced, distributed or transmitted in any form or by any means, including photocopying, recording, or other electronic or mechanical methods, without the prior written permission of the publisher, except in the case of brief quotations embodied in critical reviews and certain other noncommercial uses permitted by copyright law. For permission requests, write to the author, at: emiko.susilo@gmail.com.

Author Name
Emiko Saraswati Susilo

Illustrator Name
I Dewa Putu Berata

Publisher Name
Emiko Saraswati Susilo

Contact Information
https://emikosusilo.com

Nyepi The Day of Silence/ Emiko Saraswati Susilo —1st ed.
ISBN 978-0-9974383-1-4

Dedication
For our parents, our brothers and sisters,
and most of all for Ayu and Dodé.

# Nyepi
# The Day of Silence

By Emiko Saraswati Susilo

Illustrated by I Dewa Putu Berata

The sun was setting, and the clouds were fluffy in the sky.

Ayu and Dodé ran through the rice fields toward their home. They did NOT want to be out after the sun went down!

Tonight was the most exciting... and most scary... night of the year.

For months, the young people of the village had been working hard, building towering monsters of paper, cloth, wire, and bamboo. Now, they were big, scary "ogoh-ogoh" that would dance down the street.

When Ayu and Dodé got home, the road was crowded with grandmas, grandpas, aunts, and uncles. The big kids were excited. The musicians were ready.

Finally there was a signal - a big wooden drum was struck at the center of the village.

KU---KUL!

KU---KUL!

KU---KUL--- KUL KUL KUL!

Each 'ogoh-ogoh' was carried to the center of the village and given special offerings in the cemetery.

"What's that for?" Dodé asked Bapak.

"They are offerings. The real monsters like anger, greed, and jealousy live inside of us and all around us. We are giving them offerings. After that, we ask them to live peacefully with us."

The big kids carried them, bouncing them up and down, shouting and running. The ogoh-ogoh were many different colors and shapes and were creaking and teetering. Ayu and Dodé were SURE one of them was going to fall down or tear apart!

The musicians played big cymbals, drums, and gongs. It was like big waves crashing onto the shore - very exciting, and a tiny bit scary.

The music and shouts got louder and louder! Suddenly, it became quiet.

"What's happening?" Dodé whispered to Ayu.
"I don't know," Ayu whispered back.

All of a sudden, a man jumped out and started yelling! He yelled and waved his arms and seemed angry. Everyone listened, but no one could understand him.
He wasn't angry! He was just making silly sounds and dancing around!

Then another person jumped out and made funny arguing sounds. The musicians played music, battling with their big sounds. Finally one of the ogoh-ogoh rushed ahead, and the other one raced after it.

On the way home, everyone laughed thinking of the ogoh-ogoh stuck at the intersection.

They thought about how clever the man had been to make everyone laugh instead of fight.

He was a hero.

Ayu and Dodé woke up the next morning
to the sound of something very unusual.
It was the sound of silence.
It was Nyepi.
The Day of Silence.

Actually, it wasn't silent. When they listened, their ears began to hear many sounds!

Dodé was good at listening.
Today he heard: the birds in the trees, the chickens scratching in the yard, Grandmother's gentle footsteps, the wind in the leaves, and the stream in the rice field.

But there were no cars, motorcycles, cell phone beeps, and no TVs.
Even airplanes were silent.

Ayu sniffed. The smells were different! Normally she would smell sandalwood incense and the wood fire burning in the kitchen.
Not today.

Today, she could smell the flowers in the family temple, the damp earth, and the rain that was falling in the West.

They walked out into the family courtyard.

"Mbok Ayu..." Dodé said sleepily, calling her "Mbok" which means "big sister." She reached out to make sure he wouldn't fall off the raised patio.

They sat together. It was chilly as they watched the morning sky turn from dark purple to light pink.

Mami saw them and smiled. Bapak brought four steaming cups.

Thankfully someone had boiled water last night and put it in the big thermos. There were hibiscus flowers floating in the cups, and a bit of sugar sweetened the bright red tea.

Some people would fast and be silent all day, but that was too hard for Ayu and Dodé. They ate spicy soup and rice steamed in pandanus leaves which had been cooked the night before.

Later in the morning, Dodé peeked out of their doorway and saw the streets empty. Not a single car, motorbike, bicycle, or person was outside their house.

"Let's go play, Dodé!" giggled Ayu.

"No, Mbok Ayu. We can't go out today. It's Nyepi," said Dodé.

"Oh come on! Just for a little bit," Ayu said smiling.

"We should stay home. No one is allowed outside of their house," said Dodé seriously as he turned back into the house pulling his big sister with him.

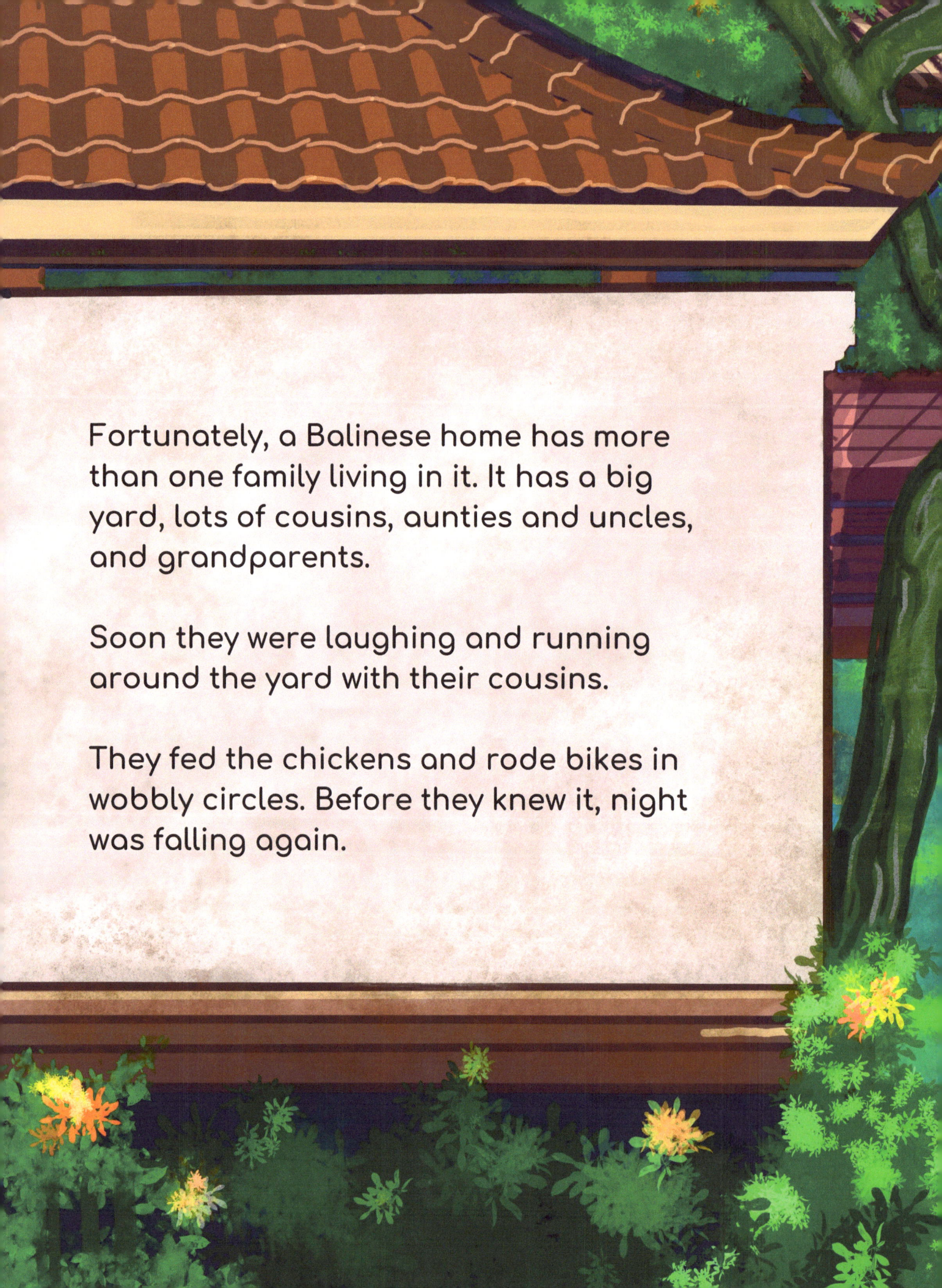

Fortunately, a Balinese home has more than one family living in it. It has a big yard, lots of cousins, aunties and uncles, and grandparents.

Soon they were laughing and running around the yard with their cousins.

They fed the chickens and rode bikes in wobbly circles. Before they knew it, night was falling again.

It grew very quiet.

No lights

No candles

No TVs

No gamelan

No street lights

No stores open.

Dodé and Ayu felt a little nervous, so they stayed right next to each other.

They could hear the crickets, frogs, and the lizards who shouted,
"TOKAAAAY....TOKAAAAAY....TOKAY- A- A- AY!"
They were so loud!

Then it got very quiet again.

It was peaceful but a little scary.

"It's so dark, Mami," Ayu whispered.
"Come sit by me, pumpkin pie. Let's look at all the stars."

They heard their neighbor's baby crying for a moment.
Soon they heard the gentle sound of someone singing quietly, and the baby stopped crying.

Suddenly, they were startled by a loud sound.

It was a motorbike driving past the house! It seemed so loud.
Why was there a motorbike and a car?

Then they smelled incense and the fire in the hearth. They heard Grandmother sweeping and Grandfather listening to his radio.

The Day of Silence was over.

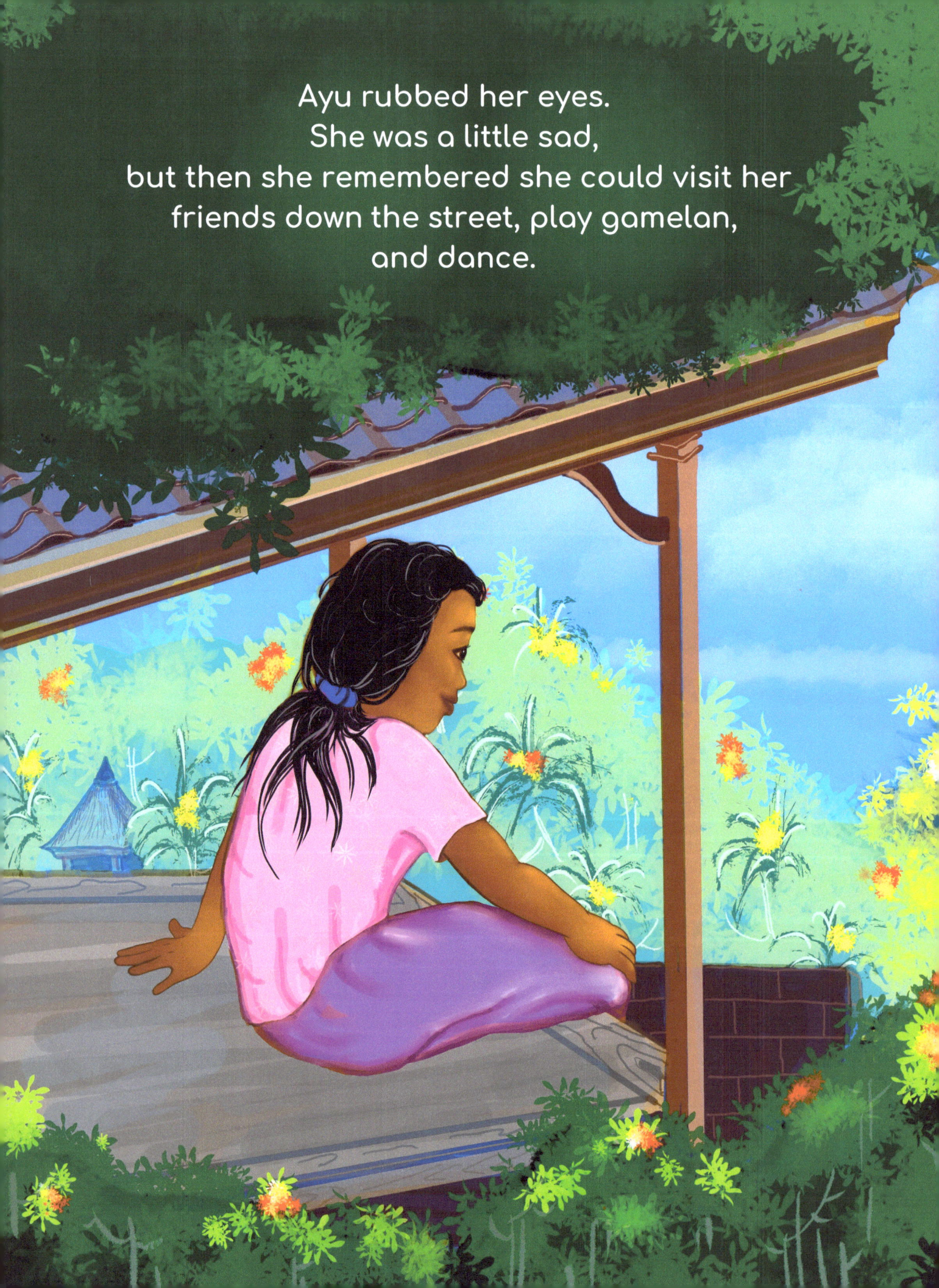

She closed her eyes and said, "Thank you, Day of Silence. I will wait for you to come again. Happy New Year."

Dodé called out to her with big eyes. "Let's gooooo!" he said, moving his hands excitedly.

He grabbed her hand, and they laughed as they raced out into the New Year!

Pronunciation:
- Ayu is pronounced like the letters: I.U.
- Dodé is pronounced: Doe - DAY.
- Nyepi is pronounced: Nyuh-PEA (rhymes with "a TREE").
- Bali rhymes with the American pronunciation of "Holly" - as in Hollywood.
- The "O" in "ogoh-ogoh" is similar to the "o" in the word "boy."

Cultural Notes:
- Nyepi is not January first. It follows a lunar calendar, so it is on a different day every year. It usually falls in March or April.
- The airport is closed on Nyepi - no flights are allowed in or out of Bali!

Surprises:
- Ayu and Dodé are real people!
- Ayu helped with the artwork in this book.
- Real life Dodé loves soccer.
- The bunny in this book is a real bunny! Her name is "Kuning."
- The black dog is also real. Her name is "Acey."

www.ingramcontent.com/pod-product-compliance
Lightning Source LLC
Chambersburg PA
CBHW041441010526
44118CB00003B/147